PRAYING THE BIBLE

— WHILE —

SAYING THE ROSARY

Scriptural Meditation For Rosary Beads

RUSSELL P. FOREMAN, JR.

ILLUSTRATOR, SISTER CATHERINE MARTIN

WESTBOW
PRESS®
A DIVISION OF THOMAS NELSON
& ZONDERVAN

WestBow Press books may be ordered through booksellers or by contacting:

WestBow Press
A Division of Thomas Nelson & Zondervan
1663 Liberty Drive
Bloomington, IN 47403
www.westbowpress.com
1 (866) 928-1240

ISBN: 978-1-9736-0532-4 (sc)
ISBN: 978-1-9736-0533-1 (e)

Library of Congress Control Number: 2017914979

Print information available on the last page.

WestBow Press rev. date: 11/16/2017

ACKNOWLEDGEMENTS

MANY THANKS TO:

FATHER DON ZEILER (PASTOR, ST GABRIEL CATHOLIC COMMUNITY) for his patience and numerous suggestions particularly in the formative years of this endeavor.

JOHN SMITH (FRIEND, FELLOW PARISHONER, BIBLE STUDY COMPANION AT ST GABRIEL'S CATHOLIC COMMUNITY) for his generous contribution of rosary resources, particularly the "audio version".

FATHER KAROPI for his radio ministry homily suggestion of "praying the Bible while saying the rosary" several years ago.

THE THIRD PERSON OF THE BLESSED TRINITY for persistence in getting me back on track during periods of distraction, and for not giving up on me, I am forever indebted and grateful.

MY WIFE BARBARA for her infinite patience with me, especially during this endeavor, her suggestions for improving the text and computer assistance without which you would not be reading this, but most especially for her biblical life of love.

MY "98 YEAR OLD" FATHER-IN-LAW WILLIAM CAREY SALASSI for his consistent patriarchal spiritual guidance, leadership and example, and for sharing his extensive biblical knowledge. As a senior approaching "centenarian" status, he advised me that when he was a youth, the Dead Sea was only a Sick Sea.

SISTER CATHERINE MARTIN, O. CARM. for gracing this publication with her God given artistic talent. Her book covers and book interior images are without equal.

MY SON, RUSTY FOREMAN, for recovering this script which seemed lost during the critical last stages of this book's completion.

PUBLISHER WESTBOW PRESS for their confidence in me.

MY BOOK COORDINATOR, TIM FITCH, for guiding me through the necessary steps to achieve this completed book; his never ending patience allowed me the space I so needed, especially during medical interruptions. Many thanks, Tim.

DEDICATION

This work is dedicated to:

BARBARA, my faithful wife going on fifty years, my number one encourager, my caretaker extraordinaire, and most importantly my soul-mate in a lifetime of biblical study.

MICHELLE, my eldest granddaughter who at an early age inquired of me about the rosary beads she noticed next to my bed and who has been a special blessing in my life. Her computer skills were a significant catalyst at critical times when this publication needed a boost.

GRANDMA ROSA BREAUX FOREMAN, my example as a young lad, who routinely prayed her rosary most faithfully.

FOREWORD

PART 1

In the words of Ignatius of Loyola as he met Francis Xavier along the Appian Way: "Greetings !!!" And I might add "Welcome to this study".

Born and raised in predominately Catholic Cajun southwest Louisiana, I attended Cathedral High School run by The Christian Brothers in Lafayette, LA, where upper grade students were required **every week** to **memorize word for word** that Sunday's Mass Gospel reading and then correctly **recite** that **biblical passage** in full to acquire a passing grade. This biblical regiment was beneficial in preparing me for the challenges associated with connecting the mass to the Bible and eventually complete the research you will encounter herein.

When more recently presented with the concept of "Praying the Bible" in a homily by Father Karopi on Catholic Radio, a natural next step, for me, was to test this hypothesis. This book is the result of meticulous biblical research produced by Father Karopi's challenge.

"Do not put out the spirit's fire…….. . Test everything……. ."
1 Thessalonians 5:19-21, page 1821 (NIV Giant Print).

The use of prayer beads for communication with God goes back to ancient times, including the Hebrew culture. The rosary is a special expression of prayer beads. It is used in the Roman Catholic Church as a specific form of meditation and prayer as Mary requested in her Fatima apparition.

It is not within the scope of this study to enumerate or explain the various times that God sent Mary to appear on earth while saying the Rosary. However, her 1531 A.D. apparition was a catalyst in the further evolution of **lay ministry**. Interestingly, my current home state of TX, has a connection to this apparition which occurred at **Tepeyac**, a hill in central Mexico (wherein Mary was referred to as **Our Lady of Guadalupe**). Mary appeared to an indigenous man named **Juan Diego**, asking him to build a church that would foster the spread of the Gospel in the Americas. As a sign of her presence, Mary left **roses blooming** in this **desert** region of Mexico.

Fast forward to El Paso, TX, today, where a **spiritual rose** is in **bloom** at **Tepeyac Institute** which trains **lay people** for ministry. It has done this for the last quarter of a century, furthering God's intention as delivered by Mary in the referenced apparition.

For a further link between the rosary and the Bible, look no further than the WWII dramatic air encounter between Catholic German, Messerschmitt ME-109 fighter pilot, Major Franz

Stigler who pressed against his rosary beads and Allied B-17 bomber pilot, Charles Brown, his hand pressing on his Bible.* This encounter had an unlikely ending as could ever be imagined, yet another link between the rosary and the Bible!

PART 2

PRAYING THE BIBLE WHILE SAYING THE ROSARY: SCRIPTURAL MEDITATION FOR ROSARY BEADS

The distinct nature of this subject and necessary attributes for successful accomplishment of what will be suggested herein is a great reminder of just how difficult it is to stay focused when in prayer. Perhaps we can relate to the following:

Once upon a time, there was an "abbey" of castle-like dimensions, built on an elevated parcel of land that dominated the nearby landscape, and was the domicile for a cloistered order of contemplative monks who never left these confines with the exception of the Abbott who was designated by rank to handle the administrative needs of the order.

With frugality and self-sufficiency a necessity, the surrounding land was farmed by share-croppers as a food supply for the abbey.

On one of his regularly scheduled field inspections, riding a magnificent thoroughbred with a silver and gold adorned pure leather saddle, the Abbott encountered a field hand bent on conversation.

It seems this laborer had become a great admirer of the magnificent abbey structure, but not more so than with the horse and the saddle now before him.

Unable to contain his enthusiasm, he petitioned the Abbott to let him join the ranks of the monks. Try as he may, the Abbott could not convince him that life in the abbey was not easy to bear: vows of poverty and chastity, an austere and regimented cloistered existence complete with hard surfaced bedding, hours given to memorizing Gregorian chants, seemingly endless choral harmony sessions with fellow monks, sleep deprivation for a daily midnight "praise devotion in Chapel", prolonged periods of meditative silence, numerous menial tasks with kitchen and barnyard duty thrown in for good measure. None of this seemed to deter the laborer. Finally, the Abbott raised the issue of a monk needing to have unwavering self-control to remain **focused** during long periods of **prayer**.

With the laborer still insistent that he could meet all of these challenges, the Abbott sought to demonstrate the difficulty of **focused prayer** by offering his prized mount to the laborer if only he could recite "The Lord's Prayer" aloud at that moment without any interruption.

The laborer wasted not a second, dropped to his knees and immediately began to pray: "Our Father who art in heaven, hallowed be thy name, thy kingdom come, thy will be done on earth as it is in heaven." Oh, excuse me Father Abbott, but does that **saddle** come with the **horse**?

---

*See "A Higher Call: An Incredible True Story of Combat and Chivalry In The War Torn Skies Of World War Two".

PART 3:

Now it is our turn to concentrate as we pray the bible while saying the rosary.

The <u>NIV Giant Print Bible</u> was selected for the biblical reference to benefit those with challenged eyesight, especially seniors, plus the biblical wording in this particular edition most resembles the prayer wording found in the Rosary recitation.

Note: If you personally prefer another Bible edition, see Book, Chapter, and Verse in the "reference and quote" column herein to follow along in the Bible edition you prefer.

Here are some suggestions for using this book. Have your Bible nearby while reading this book and saying the rosary as a ready reference to passages. There are sections included in this book for your use as a "reflection journal". Then, after a few months, reread this book to discover what new inspirations the Holy Spirit will provide at that time for you to journal.

A prayerful beginning:
Dearest Lord Jesus, May this work glorify your Name and bring the reader to a closer walk with You. Amen.

CHAPTER 1

PRAYERS FOR THE ROSARY BEADS

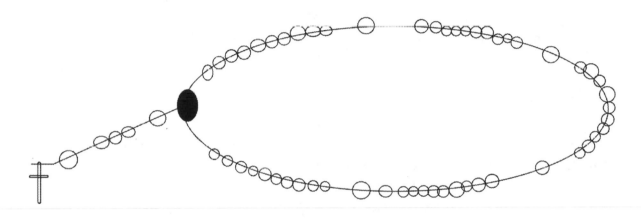

As shown in this diagram, the rosary prayer beads consist of a cross on a single chain, followed by a bead, then a cluster of three beads, and finally another single bead. This chain is then attached to a medal piece that is the beginning of a circle of five decades or sets of ten beads, each set separated by a single bead. The following prayers are said on specified beads in a predetermined sequence, which will be addressed in a later chapter.

The purpose of this section is to show that when saying/reciting these prayers (noted below) you are actually quoting/praying the Bible.

I have developed a four column table to match the prayer words of the rosary to a Bible book, chapter, and verse. In the table, for easy comparison purposes, I have also included the page number for the passage as found in the <u>NIV Giant Print Bible</u>. The last column contains a referenced passage wording from <u>Luther's Small Catechism</u>, <u>1986 Translation</u> (a Lutheran Church publication), where appropriate. The evidence for the rosary prayer words from the Bible are demonstrated in this four column comparison table.

NOTE: The Rosary PRAYER SEQUENCE is delineated in a separate section of this book. For now, here are the prayers.

A. THE HAIL MARY

Prayer Words	Biblical References and Quote	Page Number	Luther Catechism
"HAIL MARY"	Luke 1:28 The angel went to her (Mary) and said: "GREETINGS,"	1575	N/A
"FULL OF GRACE"	Luke 1:28 "YOU WHO ARE HIGHLY FAVORED!"	1575	N/A
"THE LORD IS WITH THEE"	Luke 1:28 (last sentence) "THE LORD IS WITH YOU"	1575	N/A
"BLESSED ART THOU AMONG WOMEN"	Luke 1:42 "IN A LOUD VOICE SHE (ELIZABETH) EXCLAIMED: BLESSED ARE YOU (MARY) AMONG WOMEN." AND Luke 1:48 MAGNIFICAT: (MARY'S SONG): "FROM NOW ON ALL GENERATIONS WILL CALL ME BLESSED."	1576 1576	N/A
AND BLESSED IS THE FRUIT OF THY WOMB, JESUS."	Luke 1: 41&42 "WHEN ELIZABETH HEARD MARY'S GREETING, THE BABY LEAPED IN HER WOMB, AND ELIZABETH WAS FILLED WITH THE HOLY SPIRIT. IN A LOUD VOICE SHE EXCLAIMED: BLESSED ARE YOU AMONG WOMEN AND BLESSED IS THE CHILD YOU WILL BEAR."	1576	N/A

Prayer Words	Biblical References and Quote	Page Number	Luther Catechism
"HOLY MARY"	Luke 1:46&47 MAGNIFICAT: (MARY'S SONG) AND MARY SAID: "MY SOUL GLORIFIES THE LORD AND MY SPIRIT REJOICES IN GOD MY SAVIOR."	1576	N/A
"MOTHER OF GOD"	Luke 1:30&31: "BUT THE ANGEL (GABRIEL) SAID TO HER: DO NOT BE AFRAID, MARY, YOU HAVE FOUND FAVOR WITH GOD. YOU WILL BE WITH CHILD AND GIVE BIRTH TO A SON AND YOU ARE TO GIVE HIM THE NAME JESUS."	1575	N/A
"PRAY FOR US SINNERS NOW AND AT THE HOUR OF OUR DEATH. AMEN."	N/A	N/A	N/A

Notes: The reference to "Magnificat" has its origin in the "Latin Vulgate" translation of the Bible, the opening word being MAGNIFICAT, Luke 1:46-55 (page 1576), which means GLORIFIES and is similar to a psalm while the "Latin Vulgate" for PRAISE BE, Luke 1:68-79 (page 1577), is BENEDICTUS where we get our English word BENEDICTION and is more like a prophesy. Also, GLORIA IN EXCELSIS DEO (Glory to God in the Highest), Luke 2:14 (page 1578), derives from the Latin Vulgate.

B. "THE OUR FATHER"

Prayer Words	Biblical References and Quote	Page #	Luther Catechism
"OUR FATHER WHO ART IN HEAVEN, HALLOWED BE THY NAME; THY KINGDOM COME, THY WILL BE DONE ON EARTH AS IT IS IN HEAVEN. GIVE US THIS DAY OUR DAILY BREAD AND FORGIVE US OUR TRESPASSES AS WE FORGIVE THOSE WHO TRESPASS AGAINST US	MT 6:9-13 "THIS THEN IS HOW YOU SHOULD PRAY: OUR FATHER IN HEAVEN, HALLOWED BE YOUR NAME, YOUR KINGDOM COME, YOUR WILL BE DONE ON EARTH AS IT IS IN HEAVEN. GIVE US TODAY OUR DAILY BREAD. FORGIVE US OUR DEBTS AS WE ALSO HAVE FORGIVEN OUR DEBTORS	1493	Pages 10-14: "OUR FATHER, WHO ART IN HEAVEN, HALLOWED BE THY NAME, THY KINGDOM COME, THY WILL BE DONE ON EARTH AS IT IS IN HEAVEN. GIVE US THIS DAY OUR DAILY BREAD; AND FORGIVE US OUR TRESPASSES AS WE FORGIVE THOSE WHO TRESPASS AGAINST US; AND LEAD US NOT INTO TEMPTATION BUT DELIVER US FROM EVIL. FOR THINE IS THE KINGDOM AND THE POWER AND THE GLORY FOREVER AND EVER. AMEN."
AND LEAD US NOT INTO TEMP-TATION BUT DELIVER US FROM EVIL. AMEN."	AND LEAD US NOT INTO TEMP-TATION BUT DELIVER US FROM THE EVIL ONE."		

REFLECTION:

1. **How sincerely do I believe these words?: Thy will be done on earth as it is in heaven.**

2. **What "lifestyle changes" do these specific prayer words demand of me?**

C. "THE GLORY BE"

Prayer Words	Biblical References and Quote	Page #	Luther Catechism
"GLORY BE TO THE FATHER AND TO THE SON AND TO THE HOLY SPIRIT"	EXODUS 15:1&2 "I WILL SING TO THE LORD FOR HE IS HIGHLY EXALTED... HE (THE LORD) IS MY GOD AND I WILL PRAISE HIM... AND I WILL EXALT HIM."	106	N/A
"AS IT WAS IN THE BEGINNING, IS NOW, AND EVER SHALL BE, WORLD WITHOUT END. AMEN."	"Jesus Christ is the same yesterday and today and forever." HEBREWS 13:8 (p.1857) (PRAYERFUL ACKNOWLEDGEMENT THAT GOD IS THE SAME "YESTERDAY, TODAY AND TOMORROW"); the wording in the Second Addition of THE DIVINE LITURGY (in GREEK and ENGLISH), A Guide for Christian Worshipers by Rev. Nicholas Elias in 1948 (Page 73), the wording is: "Now and forever, and from all ages to all ages. Amen."		
	"Day and night they never stop saying: Holy, holy, holy is the Lord God Almighty, who was, and is, and is to come." (Revelation 4:8).	1891	N/A

REFLECTION:

1. How often during my busy day do I pause to "lift praise to my sovereign Lord"?

2. Write down an adjustment I can make to my daily schedule to put God first:

D. "THE APOSTLE'S CREED"

Prayer Words	Biblical References and Quote	Page #	Luther Catechism
"I BELIEVE IN GOD, THE FATHER ALMIGHTY, CREATOR OF HEAVEN AND EARTH, AND IN JESUS CHRIST, HIS ONLY SON, OUR LORD, WHO WAS CONCEIVED BY THE HOLY SPIRIT, BORN OF THE VIRGIN MARY, SUFFERED UNDER PONTIUS PILOT, WAS CRUCIFIED, DIED AND WAS BURIED; HE DECENDED INTO HELL; ON THE THIRD DAY HE ROSE AGAIN FROM THE DEAD.	N/A	N/A	PAGES 7-9 THE CREED: I BELIEVE IN ONE GOD, THE FATHER ALMIGHTY, MAKER OF HEAVEN AND EARTH. AND IN JESUS CHRIST, HIS ONLY SON, OUR LORD, WHO WAS CONCEIVED BY THE HOLY SPIRIT, BORN OF THE VIRGIN MARY, SUFFERED UNDER PONTIUS PILATE, WAS CRUCIFIED, DIED AND WAS BURIED. HE DECENDED INTO HELL. THE THIRD DAY HE ROSE AGAIN FROM THE DEAD. HE ASCENDED INTO HEAVEN AND SITS
I BELIEVE IN THE HOLY SPIRIT, THE HOLY CATHOLIC CHURCH, THE COMMUNION OF SAINTS, THE FORGIVENESS OF SINS, THE RESURRECTION OF THE BODY, AND LIFE EVERLASTING. AMEN."	N/A	N/A	AT THE RIGHT HAND OF GOD, THE FATHER ALMIGHTY. FROM THENCE HE WILL COME TO JUDGE THE LIVING AND THE DEAD. I BELIEVE IN THE HOLY SPIRIT, THE COMMUNION OF SAINTS, THE FORGIVENESS OF SINS, THE RESURECTION OF THE BODY AND LIFE EVERLASTING. AMEN."

OPTIONAL PRAYER (SUGGESTED BY MARY DURING ONE OF HER MANY APPARATIONS) WHICH MAY BE SAID AT THE END OF EACH DECADE FOLLOWING THE "GLORY BE":

Prayer Words	Biblical References and Quote	Page #	Luther Catechism
OH MY JESUS, FORGIVE US OUR SINS, SAVE US FROM THE FIRES OF HELL.	1JOHN1:9: "IF WE CONFESS OUR SINS, HE IS FAITHFUL AND JUST AND WILL FORGIVE US OUR SINS AND PURIFY US FROM ALL UNRIGHTEOUSNESS."	1876	NA
AND LEAD ALL SOULS TO HEAVEN, ESPECIALLY THOSE IN MOST NEED OF THY MERCY.	1JOHN 2:1 "…BUT IF ANYBODY DOES SIN, WE HAVE ONE WHO SPEAKS TO THE FATHER IN OUR DEFENSE----JESUS CHRIST, THE RIGHTEOUS ONE."	1876	N/A

CHAPTER 2

AN INTERESTING COMPARISON

The following pages show the similarity of the Apostle's Creed with the Nicene Creed of 325 A.D, in Nicea.

THE APOSTLE'S CREED:	THE NICENE CREED:
I believe in God, the Father almighty, Creator of heaven and earth, and in Jesus Christ, his only Son, our Lord, who was conceived by the Holy Spirit, born of the Virgin Mary, suffered under Pontius Pilot, was crucified, died and was buried; he descended into hell ;on the third day he rose again from the dead. I believe in the Holy Spirit, the holy catholic Church, the communion of saints, the forgiveness of sins, and the resurrection of the body, and life everlasting. Amen.	I believe in one God, the Father almighty, maker of heaven and earth, of all things visible and invisible. I believe in one Lord Jesus Christ, the only Begotten Son of God, born of the Father before all ages. God from God, Light from Light, true God from true God, begotten, not made, consubstantial with the Father; through him all things were made. For us men and for our salvation, he came down from heaven, and by the Holy Spirit was incarnate of the Virgin Mary and became man.

THE APOSTLE'S CREED:	THE NICENE CREED:
	For our sake, he was crucified under Pontius Pilot; he suffered death and was buried, and rose again on the the third day in accordance with the Scriptures. He ascended into heaven and is seated at the right hand of the Father. He will come again in glory to judge the living and the dead and his kingdom will have no end. I believe in the Holy Spirit, the Lord, the giver of life, who proceeds from the Father and the Son,who with the Father and the Son is adored and glorified, who has spoken through the prophets. I believe in one, holy, catholic and apostolic church. I confess one baptism for the forgiveness of sins and I look forward to the resurrection of the dead and the life of the world to come. Amen.

NOTE: The PROFESSION OF FAITH recited in the Catholic Mass is the NICENE CREED, word for word.

CHAPTER 3

THE MYSTERIES OF THE ROSARY

Prayers on the five decades of beads are organized into four different meditations called mysteries, which reflect certain events or lessons in the life of Jesus, our Lord.

The four mysteries of the rosary are:

1. **Joyful**
2. **Sorrowful**
3. **Glorious**
4. **Luminous**

Each mystery consists of five decades (or five sets of ten beads) for praying and meditation of that mystery. Each decade of that mystery has a specific meditation that relates to that mystery. Biblical references and images are included for each of the five decades of each of the four mysteries for easy meditation. Normally, only one mystery at a time is prayed on the rosary during any given prayer time, versus all four mysteries at the same time or in a single prayer session.

The mysteries are prayed and meditated on the beads strung on the circular chain. Each decade is separated by a single bead. Each decade is a particular lesson or event that teaches about the life of Jesus and relates to the mystery that you are reciting/meditating.

While using this book to meditate on a mystery, I would suggest that you say the prayers for the decade, then read the Biblical passage/passages for that decade. Before moving to the next decade, pray about what you have just read and put yourself into the scene as an onlooker. Pray that Christ will speak to you as you listen and pray.

PRAYER SEQUENCE ON THE BEADS

DETERMINE in advance and ANNOUNCE which Mystery you plan to meditate (example: THE JOYFUL MYSTERIES).

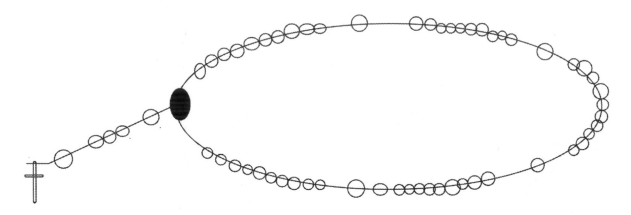

On the cross, make the "SIGN OF THE CROSS" and pray the "APOSTLE'S CREED".

On the first bead after the cross, pray the "OUR FATHER".

On the following three beads, pray the "HAIL MARY".

On the last bead, pray the "GLORY BE".

FROM THIS POINT ON (see black metallic oval on the above diagram), YOU ARE PRAYING THE FIVE DECADES OF THE BEADS (FIVE SETS OF TEN BEADS SEPARATED BY A SINGLE BEAD).

On the flat metallic connection (the black oval in above diagram), ANNOUNCE the first DECADE meditation (example: THE ANNUNCIATION), and pray the "OUR FATHER".

On the next ten beads, pray the "HAIL MARY" while meditating on the first decade of the mystery as found in the Bible passages.

Then pray the "GLORY BE" on the bead-less portion of chain following the last bead of the decade. Then pray (OPTIONAL) "OH MY JESUS, FORGIVE US OUR SINS" prayer also on this same bead-less chain.

Use the next "single" bead to announce the SECOND DECADE (example: THE VISITATION) and pray the "Our Father".

Repeat the same SEQUENCE OF PRAYERS as for the "FIRST DECADE" while meditating on the SECOND DECADE biblical passages.

Do the same for the "THIRD, FOURTH, AND FIFTH DECADES", while meditating on each of their Biblical passages. Use the single bead separating each decade to announce the next decade and pray the "Our Father".

NOTE:

The "Legionaries of Christ" offer a slightly modified version to what is noted above. Specifically:

1. At the very BEGINNING, after the "Apostle's Creed", the "Our Father" and three "Hail Mary's", the "Glory Be" is omitted on the last bead, replaced by "announcing the first mystery".
2. The rosary concludes with the "Hail Holy Queen" prayer followed by "the sign of the cross".

Because this "modification" goes beyond the scope of this examination, those so inclined can pursue more in depth at www.LegionionairesofChrist.org or 1-800-532-7478.

And for information on the "Divine Mercy Chaplet" attributable to **St** Maria Faustina, Marian Fathers of the Immaculate Conception of the B.V.M. can be reached at 1-800-462-7426, their number for orders. The Chaplet of St Anthony has 13 Our Fathers, Hail Mary's, and Glory Be's with 13 optional invocations to say before each Our Father, Hail Mary, and Glory Be. The number 13 is said to coincide with what has been called "The Miraculous Responsory". While the booklet "Companion Prayers (A Guide to Prayer from the Companions of St Anthony)" provides more detail, it is beyond the scope of this publication.

CHAPTER 4

IMAGES FOR THE FOUR MYSTERIES

On the following pages, each provided decade image focuses on a particular mystery, and is followed by a Biblical reference source on the succeeding page . This allows you to connect each decade image with the corresponding Biblical reference. Space is provided to record your reflections.

THE MYSTERIES AND THEIR DECADES

Joyful Mysteries: Annunciation, Visitation, Nativity, Presentation, Finding in the Temple

Sorrowful Mysteries: Agony in the Garden, Scourging of Jesus at the Pillar, Jesus Is Crowned with Thorns, Jesus Carries His Cross, The Crucifixion

Glorious Mysteries: Resurrection, Ascension, Descent of the Holy Spirit, Assumption, Coronation of the Blessed Virgin Mary

Luminous Mysteries: Baptism of Jesus, Wedding at Cana, The Proclamation of the Kingdom, Transfiguration, Jesus Institutes the Holy Eucharist

The Joyful

Mysteries

of

The Rosary

1. THE ANNUNCIATION

Annunciation Biblical Reference Source: Luke 1:26-38 and Matthew 1: 18-25.

REFLECTION:

1. How would I react if an Angel appeared to me out of nowhere?

2. Do you think Mary's readily acceptance of God's will was in any way due to her lifelong predisposition of obedience and openness to God's will?

2. THE VISITATION

Visitation Biblical Reference Source: Luke 1:39-44

REFLECTION:

1. How do I envision the enthusiasm that must have engulfed Mary at the thought of visiting her cousin Elizabeth with the recent revelation that Elizabeth was now pregnant in a culture that looked down on barren women?

2. What must have been Mary's mode of travel over desert sands to visit Elizabeth. Do I envision her on a camel...a donkey...on foot?

3. What distance did she have to travel? Any oasis along the way?

3. THE NATIVITY

Nativity Biblical Reference Source: Luke 2: 1-20, Matthew 1:18-25 and John 1: 14.

REFLECTION:

If I were present as a shepherd during the Nativity, what would be my reaction to this never-before-experience I am now confronted with?

4. THE PRESENTATION

Presentation Biblical Reference Source: Luke 2:22-24

REFLECTION:

How much faith was required of Mary and Joseph of limited financial and travel resources, that God would provide all their needs, to faithfully fulfill this important Jewish obligation of "presentation"?

5. FINDING IN THE TEMPLE

Finding In The Temple Biblical Reference Source: Luke 2:41-50

REFLECTION:

How do I reconcile Mary's concern in not finding Jesus in the caravan versus His response that He had to be about His Father's business?

The Sorrowful Mysteries of The Rosary

1. THE AGONY IN THE GARDEN

Agony in the Garden Biblical Reference Source:
Matthew 26:36-49, Mark 14: 32-42, Luke 26:39-46 and John 18: 1-9.

REFLECTION:

1. Did I agonize with Jesus as I meditated on how He struggled to weigh what lay ahead for Him?

2. Did I at any point sense a feeling of "abandonment" during this scenario?

3. Being also present in the Garden that night, with full knowledge of what lay ahead, would I have been as obedient as Jesus was to God's will ?

4. Being as tired as the Apostles appeared to be that night, would my efforts at prayer requested by my Lord improve any on the recorded apostles' results? Or would my human desires prevail?

2. THE SCOURGING OF JESUS AT THE PILLAR

The Scourging at the Pillar Biblical Reference Source:
Matthew 27: 26, Mark 15:15, Luke 22: 63-65 and John 19:1.

REFLECTION:

If you've seen Mel Gibson's depiction of the "scourging" in his movie "The Passion", did any of those bloody images resurface upon your reflection of this horrible "cat-o-nine-tails" whipping style used by the Romans?

3. JESUS IS CROWNED WITH THORNS

The Crowning With Thorns Biblical Reference Source:
Matthew 27: 27-30, Mark 15: 16-20, and John 19:1-3.

REFLECTION:

1. Did you at all imagine the pain of a pointed thorn pressing against and entering your head as Jesus must have felt at that moment? Any "sympathy" pain?

2. How would this feeling compare with you viewing the physician entering your patient room brandishing a syringe with a significant "needle" obviously intended for you and ready for it's intended use? Get the point?

3. Do you think perhaps Jesus (who is most worthy of our respect) felt more demeaned by the insults thrown His way by His Roman torturers versus the physical pain He endured?

4. JESUS CARRIES
HIS CROSS

Jesus Carries His Cross Biblical Reference Source:
Matthew 27: 32-33, Luke 23: 26-31, and John 19:17.

REFLECTION:

1. Any splinters from the cross piercing His already bloodied and bruised body, especially resulting from the "scourging", adding to His torment?

2. Any "blisters" forming on hands of Jesus from handling the cross?

3. Realizing the complete extent of humiliation and physical suffering my Lord endured, even before His death on the cross, as a result of my sin, what commitment will I make to God today in appreciation for my salvation?

4. Since God loves me UNCONDITIONALLY (AGAPE LOVE), how should I appropriately respond?

5. THE CRUCIFIXION

The Crucifixion Biblical Reference Sources:
John 19:18, Matthew 27:45-56, Mark 15: 33-40 and Luke 23: 26-49.

REFLECTION:

Ponder the fact that the crucifixion is the ultimate reason Christ came to earth: to provide for our salvation. Give thanks to God for His overwhelming and eternal love for us.

The Glorious Mysteries of The Rosary

1. THE RESURRECTION

Resurrection Biblical Reference Source:
Matthew 28: 1-7, Mark 16: 1-20, Luke 24: 1-12 and John 20: 1-9.

REFLECTION:

1. Ponder that Christ's resurrection validates that Jesus is who He says He is; thus His words as documented in both the Old and New Testaments are true.

2. Remember that Christ is still living today, and give praise and glory to God, our Father. This is His promise to us: eternal life with Him.

2. THE ASCENSION

Ascension Biblical Reference Source: Mark 16: 14-20, Luke 24:50-53, and Acts 1: 1-11

REFLECTION:

1. **Where did Jesus indicate the Apostles were to be His witnesses subsequent to His ascension?**

2. **Are you willing to be a witness for Christ?**

3. THE DESCENT OF THE HOLY SPIRIT

Descent of the Holy Spirit Biblical Reference Source: Acts 2: 1-4

REFLECTION:

1. **Ponder the day of Pentecost as though you were present.**

2. **What are your thoughts on the roaring winds and the "tongues of fire"?**

4. THE ASSUMPTION

The Assumption Reference Source: church history and Revelation 12.

REFLECTION:

Ponder this chapter in Revelation and record your thoughts.

5. THE CORONATION OF THE BLESSED VIRGIN MARY

**The Coronation of the Blessed Virgin Mary Reference Source:
Revelation 4: 4, 9-11 and church history.**

REFLECTION:

Ponder the good news that all followers of Jesus shall receive our personal crown if we believe in HIM and remain faithful by submitting to His will as Mary did, our ideal example to follow.

The Luminous Mysteries of The Rosary

AKA "THE MYSTERIES OF LIGHT"

1. THE BAPTISM OF JESUS

Baptism of Jesus Biblical Reference Source:
Matthew 2: 13-16, Mark 1: 9-11, and John 1: 29-34.

REFLECTION:

1. Do you perceive Jesus' baptism as a point of diminishing role for John the Baptist and elevation of Jesus as Messiah?

2. How do YOU recognize Jesus as the Messiah?

2. THE WEDDING AT CANA

Wedding At Cana Biblical Reference Source: John 2: 1-11

REFLECTION:

Mary instructed the wine stewards to do whatever Jesus tells you. Are we as obedient as the wine stewards in doing what Jesus instructs us to do? Is what He is asking too tedious, mundane, or difficult?

The reign of God is at hand! Reform your lives and believe in the Gospel! Mk-1:15

3. THE PROCLAMATION OF THE KINGDOM

Proclamation of the Kingdom Biblical Reference Source:
Matthew 4:23-7:28, Mark 4: 1-34, Luke 4:42-44, 3:1-21 and John 7:14-44.

REFLECTION:

As you internalize eternal, spiritual life based on the Good News delivered by Jesus, how JOYOUS is that?

4. THE TRANSFIGURATION OF JESUS

Transfiguration Biblical Reference Source: Matthew 17: 1-8, Mark 9:2-8 and Luke 9: 28-36.

REFLECTION:

Ponder the mountain top "joys" of your life in contrast with your daily "valley" challenges. Do your daily experiences correspond with Peter's desire to remain on the mountain top rather than return to the every day valley challenges?

5. THE LAST SUPPER
THE HOLY EUCHARIST

The Last Supper Biblical Reference Source:
1 Corinthians 11: 23-29, Mark 14: 12-24, Matthew 26: 26-39, and Luke 33: 14-20.

REFLECTION:

Ponder on what a beautiful remembrance God continually provides His followers reflecting His eternal LOVE for us.

ON PAGE 1578 (NIV GIANT PRINT), LUKE 2:19 TELLS US: **"BUT MARY TREASURED UP ALL THESE THINGS AND PONDERED THEM IN HER HEART."**

CHAPTER 5
CONCLUSION

REFLECTION:

1. As a result of this "overall" study, have I grown spiritually closer to God?

How?

Why?

2. During my meditations, what "most" captured my imagination?

Thoughtfully examine why you felt drawn to this particular scene. For best outcomes, remain sincere.

Finally, commit to a certain time daily to further examine where the Holy Spirit is leading you.

My exclusive time with God each day shall begin at__: AM or PM and continue for at least the following amount of time:_____.

No matter how you answer the question below, my prayer is that you were open to the Holy Spirit's guidance through the contents of <u>PRAYING THE BIBLE WHILE SAYING THE ROSARY</u>.

So, was Father Karopi correct?

I provide. You decide.

FOLLOWUP ASSIGNMENT

In a few months, challenge yourself to reread this book and journal. In particular, what did you notice in the followup reading that had not occurred to you reading it initially. Allow the Holy Spirit to highlight God's message for you then, in addition to His message to you during your initial reading.

ABOUT THE AUTHOR

Russ is a 73 year old, Louisiana native. He is a Texas resident for the past 31 years, and a retired insurance executive. He has participated in 37 CONSECUTIVE years of retreats at MANRESA in Convent, LA, which is run by the Jesuits (Society of Jesus). He is a self described "transplanted Cajun". Russ credits his Creator for survival of six stint implants, three strokes, a triple heart bypass, pacemaker implant and a mild heart attack. He is ever grateful for the time Almighty God has afforded him on this earth (including this book's completion). Russ joined the Bill Bryan American Legion West McKinney (TX) Post 110 as the CHARTER CHAPLAIN MEMBER. In 2010, subsequent to his dance performing days, Russ published a book on "tap dancing" entitled: THE SHIM SHAM (NATIONAL ANTHEM OF TAP): A BRIEF HISTORY AND DANCE NOTES. He published a second edition in 2015.

After prayerful consideration pursuant to the Holy Spirit's prompting, Russ's detailed findings are laid out herein for your study. May the Holy Spirit be your guide as you PRAY THE BIBLE through Prayerful Meditation of the Rosary.

Author as a young Scholar

Author currently.

PHOTOS OF MANRESA, AUTHOR'S JESUIT RETREAT SITE:

While these photos provide glimpses of Manresa's unique architecture and breathtaking grounds, the best way to describe Manresa verbally would be a reflection of how Manresa views itself:

There is a place on the Mississippi River halfway between New Orleans and Baton Rouge, LA, in Convent, LA, where men trade the clamor of the city for silence and solitude. It's where nobody talks to anybody but everybody talks to God amid beautiful architecture, spacious lawns and the peaceful shade of giant live oak trees, birds chirping their delightful songs of praise, not to mention the sumptuous meals provided retreatants. Manresa, a Jesuit retreat house, is situated on approximately 130 acres in aptly named New Orleans Plantation Country.

While Manresa is a place where many friendships are made and annually renewed, the key to these retreats is SILENCE; praying to God is important but listening to what God has to say to you is more important. SILENCE achieves this desired outcome, for prayer is indeed a two way conversation. We need to stop and listen.

I've been blessed by God and encouraged by my wife, Barbara, to attend 37 CONSECUTIVE retreats here and developed many long term friendships, all the while expanding my walk with our Savior and Lord.

While my declining health determined the date of my last retreat, over many years, Manresa retreats worked wonders for me and I highly recommend attending one . Go to the Manresa website and find details for attending a retreat there. The popularity of these retreats mean each available opening comes at a premium. So don't delay because experiencing God in nature and in the contemplation of His word is paramount.

Many blessings to Manresa Director Tim Murphy for his support of this book and kind cooperation.

MANRESA
on the Mississippi
FOR THE GREATER GLORY OF GOD

ABOUT THE ILLUSTRATOR

Some background on the religious order to which Illustrator Sister Catherine Martin belongs. Facts contained in a brochure compiled by the Congregation of Our Lady of Mount Carmel, provide the following biblical background to the congregation:

"Mount Carmel is the biblical site where the prophet Elijah battled the 450 prophets of Baal in a public spiritual contest which led to their defeat (1 Kings 18:19-40). Mount Carmel can be found on the Mediterranean coast of Israel overlooking the city of Haifa, which rises 1742 feet above sea level. In Hebrew "Carmel" means "the garden", for it is known to be covered with blooming flowers, flowering shrubs, and fragrant herbs.

The title of Mary as Our Lady of Mount Carmel can be traced back to hermits who lived on the renowned and blessed mountain at the time of the Old Testament. This austere and pious community prayed in expectation of the coming of the Virgin-Mother whom they believed would bring salvation to humankind. They believed that, like prophet Elijah, who ascended the mountain of Carmel to pray to God who '… went up to Carmel, crouched down to the earth, and put his head between his knees' (1Kings 18:42), for the salvation of Israel which was suffering a tremendous drought during this time. Elijah persevered in prayers and many times sent his servant to the mountain top to see any sign of foreboding rain. Elijah did not waiver in his confidence in God; on the seventh attempt of sending his servant he found that 'There is a cloud as small as a man's hand rising from the sea' (1Kings 18:44). Soon after, a drenching rain fell upon the parched land and the people of Israel were saved'."

Sister Catherine is a life long educator and artist for the Congregation. I thank God for her faith, friendship, generosity in time and effort, and insight as expressed in the illustrations and covers for this book.